Safety in the Neighborhood

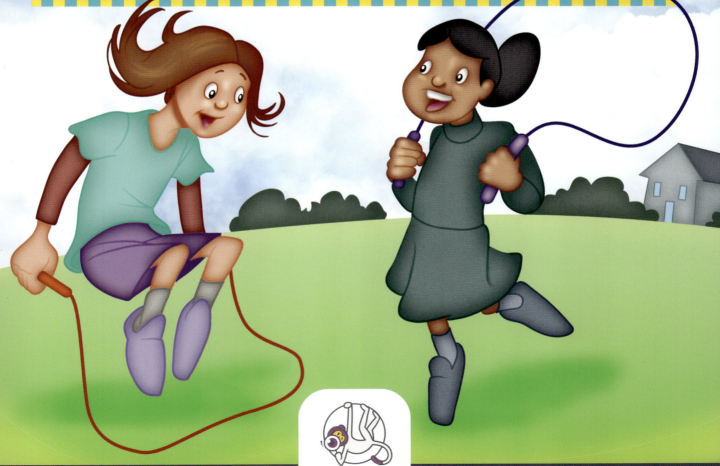

BY SUSAN KESSELRING   childsworld.com   ILLUSTRATED BY DAN McGEEHAN

Published by The Child's World®
800-599-READ • childsworld.com

Copyright © 2025 by The Child's World®
All rights reserved. No part of this book may be reproduced or utilized in any form or by any means without written permission from the publisher.

ISBN Information
9781503894037 (Reinforced Library Binding)
9781503895096 (Portable Document Format)
9781503895911 (Online Multi-user eBook)
9781503896734 (Electronic Publication)

LCCN
2024942720

Printed in the United States of America

ABOUT THE AUTHOR
Susan Kesselring loves children, books, nature, and her family. She teaches K-1 students in a progressive charter school down a little country lane in Castle Rock, Minnesota. She is the mother of five daughters and lives in Apple Valley, Minnesota with her husband and a crazy springer spaniel named Lois Lane.

ABOUT THE ILLUSTRATOR
Dan McGeehan spent his younger years as an actor, author, playwright, and editor. Now he spends his days drawing, and he is much happier.

TABLE OF CONTENTS

CHAPTER ONE
Safety In Your Neighborhood . . . 4

CHAPTER TWO
Crossing the Street . . . 7

CHAPTER THREE
Nearby Nature . . . 8

CHAPTER FOUR
Animal Neighbors . . . 11

CHAPTER FIVE
Getting Lost . . . 14

CHAPTER SIX
Strangers . . . 17

Neighborhood Safety Rules . . . 20
Wonder More . . . 21
Neighborhood Safety Hunt . . . 22
Glossary . . . 23
Find Out More . . . 24
Index . . . 24

CHAPTER 1

Safety In Your Neighborhood

What's fun to do in your neighborhood? Isn't playing with friends great? Do you ever get a sundae at the ice cream shop? Or do you find cool books at the library?

You play in your neighborhood all the time. Learn a few simple rules, and you can have fun and stay safe close to home.

Hi! I'm Buzz B. Safe. Watch for me! I'll show you how to be safe in your neighborhood.

Feeling safe in your own neighborhood is important.

A crosswalk is a marked path for walkers crossing a road. It is usually marked with white lines on the road. Whenever possible, cross a street at a crosswalk.

CHAPTER 2

Crossing the Street

Does your neighborhood have a lot of streets? You know not to play in the street. But what if you need to cross it to get to your friend's house?

Have an adult help you. Find a safe place to cross. You should be able to see far down in both directions. Look both ways for cars. When the coast is clear, walk carefully across the street. Keep your head up and eyes and ears alert for cars.

CHAPTER 3

Nearby Nature

Are there woods in your neighborhood? Playing in the woods can be fun, but it is easy to get lost among the trees.

A parent will know if it is safe to play in the woods. If it is, stay near the edge of the trees instead of playing deep in the woods. Then you can always find your way out.

When playing in the woods, keep a small flashlight in your pocket. When it starts to get dark, you'll be able to see.

Staying near the edge of the woods while playing makes it easier to find your way out.

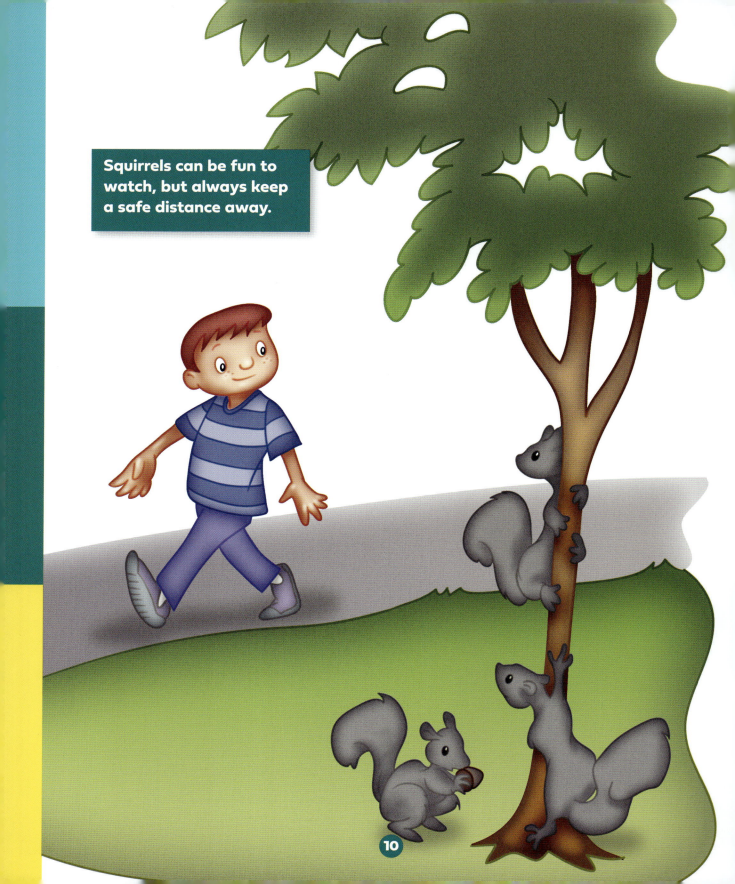

CHAPTER 4

Animal Neighbors

It's so fun to watch wild animals in your neighborhood. But avoid feeding squirrels, raccoons, or any other wild guests. Keep your distance, too. These animals need their space.

Stay away from injured and dead animals. Tell an adult about them instead.

*If a wild animal bites or scratches you, tell an adult right away. Some animals can give you **diseases**. You might need to see a doctor.*

Do you love to pet dogs? Just remember to always ask the dog's owner first. The dog might not be safe to touch. If the owner says it is okay, let the dog smell you first. Then you can pet the dog gently on its chest or under its chin.

Letting a dog sniff your hand is a good way to let the animal get to know you before you pet it.

Stray animals can sometimes be very sick.

If you see a **stray**, you might want to help. But don't get too close to it or try to catch it. Instead, have a parent call the police or an **animal shelter**.

What if a stray dog runs toward you? Don't run away. You should act like a tree. Stare straight ahead and stand very still. If the dog looks like it will bite you, throw something. The dog will chase after what you threw. Then run away as fast as you can.

Chapter 5
Getting Lost

It's possible to lose your parents in a crowd or a store. **Memorize** your address and your parents' phone numbers. Knowing these will help you get home if you are lost.

These numbers might be hard to remember at first, though. While you're learning, write them on a piece of paper. Attach the paper to the inside of your backpack or keep it in your pocket.

Stay where you are when you are lost. Look around for your parents. Call out for them too, even if you are somewhere quiet.

If you still cannot find your parents, tell an adult you are lost. Find a police officer or a worker at a store. Or, find a family and ask one of the parents for help. Before you know it, you will find your parents!

Getting lost can be scary. Try to stay calm.

Most strangers are good people. But you cannot tell by looking at a person if he or she is someone you can trust.

CHAPTER 6

Strangers

When you're lost, strangers can help you. But the rules for strangers are different when it's not an **emergency**. If a stranger offers you a ride, candy, or gifts, run away. Go home or to a place with other adults.

Never go anywhere with a stranger, even if a stranger says he or she is a friend of your family. And always tell your parents if a stranger bothers you.

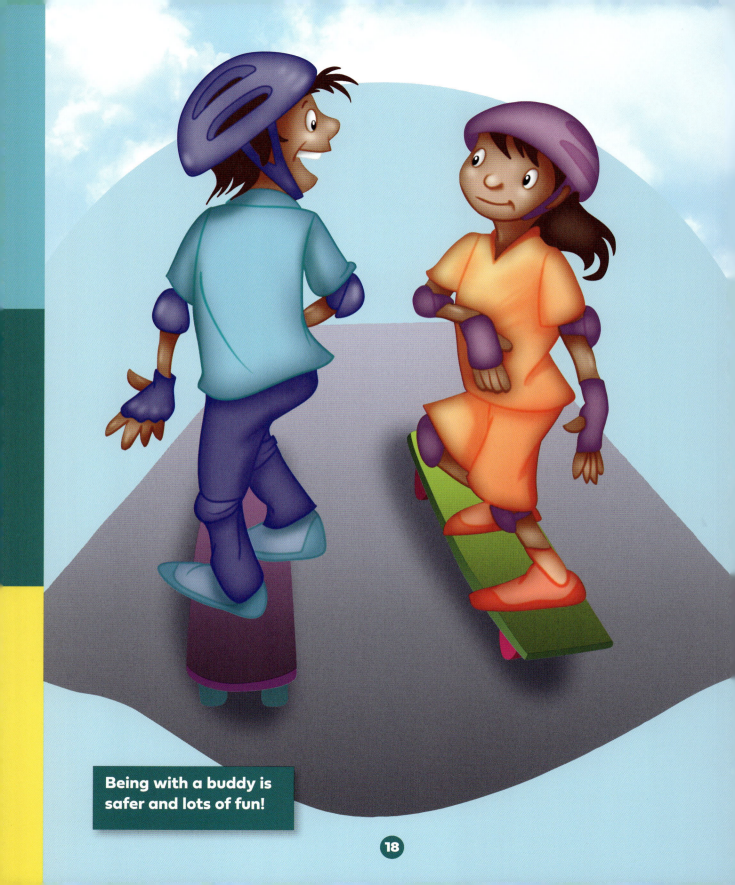

Being with a buddy is safer and lots of fun!

Always take a friend with you when you are out in the neighborhood. It is safer than going out alone. You can play together and help each other if you have any problems. With a neighborhood buddy, you can stay safe and have fun!

Never climb fences in your neighborhood. Fences are there to keep people out of spaces. If you lose a ball or kite behind a fence, ask the fence owner to get it for you.

Neighborhood Safety Rules

- Look both ways before crossing the street. Only cross when no cars are coming.
- Do not get close to wild or stray animals.
- Always ask before petting a neighbor's dog, cat, or other pet.
- Do not play in streets or go far into the woods.
- Learn your phone number, address, and your parents' names and phone numbers.
- If you are lost, call out for help. Stay where you are, too.
- Never go anywhere with a stranger.
- Bring a buddy when you go out in the neighborhood.

Wonder More

Wondering about New Information

How much did you know about neighborhood safety before you read this book? What new information did you learn? Write down three new facts that this book taught you. Was the new information surprising? Why or why not?

Wondering How It Matters

Why is it important to know your neighbors and recognize people who live around you? How can this help keep you safe?

Wondering Why

Why is it important to always look both ways before crossing a street, even if you don't see any cars?

Ways to Keep Wondering

After reading this book, what questions do you have about neighborhood safety? What can you do to learn more about it?

Neighborhood Safety Hunt

Search for safety—and dangers—in your neighborhood.

You will need:
- A marker, pen, or pencil
- A list of safety items on a piece of paper. Some ideas:
    - a crosswalk
    - a "Beware of Dog" sign
    - a stop sign
    - cracked sidewalk
    - a "Neighborhood Watch" sign

Instructions:
Take your list and a marker, pen, or pencil and walk around your neighborhood with a parent or friend. See how many things you can check off your safety list. If you see dangerous items, tell an adult right away!

Neighborhood Safety Hunt
- ☐ crosswalk
- ☐ "Beware of Dog" sign
- ☐ stop sign
- ☐ cracked sidewalk
- ☐ "Neighborhood Watch" sign

Glossary

animal shelter (AN-uh-mul SHEL-tur): An animal shelter is a place where lost or unwanted pets stay until they find homes. Have a parent call an animal shelter if you find a stray.

diseases (due-ZEE-zes): Diseases are kinds of illnesses. Some animals can give people diseases.

emergency (eh-MUR-jun-see): An emergency is a sudden situation that needs to be dealt with right away. It's okay to talk to a stranger if it's an emergency.

memorize (MEM-uh-ryz): If you memorize something, you learn it by heart. It's good to memorize your address and parents' full names and phone numbers.

stray (STRAY): A stray is an animal that is lost or has no owner. Do not go close to a stray.

Find Out More

In the Library

Feder, Yael. *The Safety Book—Strangers and Dangers*. New York, NY: Schocken Children's Books, 2022.

Geisler, Dagmar. *If I Get Lost: Stay Put, Remain Calm, and Ask for Help*. New York, NY: Sky Pony Press, 2020.

Lambert, Violet. *The Little Pedestrian's Guide: Traffic Rules*. Independently Published, 2024.

On the Web

Visit our Web site for links about neighborhood safety:
childsworld.com/links

Note to Parents, Teachers, and Librarians: We routinely verify our Web links to make sure they are safe and active sites. So encourage your readers to check them out!

Index

adults, 13, 17
bites, 11, 13
cars, 7
crosswalks, 6
dogs, 12, 13
emergency, 17
fence, 19
flashlight, 8

friends, 4, 7, 17, 19
lost, 8, 14, 15, 17
parents, 8, 13, 14, 15, 17
phone number, 14
playing, 4, 7, 8, 9, 19
police, 13, 15
raccoons, 11
run, 13, 17

strangers, 16, 17
stray, 13
street, 6, 7
squirrels, 10, 11
trees, 8, 13
woods, 8, 9